JESUS LOVES YOU

Contact Us:

✉ MyBibleWorkbooks@gmail.com

📷 Projectkingdomcome

f Projectkingdomcome

PROJECT KINGDOM COME
ISBN 978-1-961786-08-0

Get The Entire Workbook Series!

...male and female He created them. Genesis 1:27
THE BOOK OF
GENESIS
BIBLE-BASED WORKBOOK
Take an adventure into the amazing Book of Genesis and test your knowledge as you go!
PROJECT KINGDOM COME

Sun, stand still. Joshua 10:12
THE BOOKS OF
EXODUS & JOSHUA
BIBLE-BASED WORKBOOK
Take an adventure into the amazing Books of Exodus and Joshua and test your knowledge as you go!
PROJECT KINGDOM COME

And they anointed David king over the house of Judah. 2nd Samuel 2:4
THE BOOKS OF
I & II SAMUEL
BIBLE-BASED WORKBOOK
Take an adventure into the amazing Books of 1st and 2nd Samuel and test your knowledge as you go!
PROJECT KINGDOM COME

and he shall come and sit on my throne and be king. 1st Kings 1:35
THE BOOKS OF
I & II KINGS
BIBLE-BASED WORKBOOK
Take an adventure into the amazing Books of 1st and 2nd Kings and test your knowledge as you go!
PROJECT KINGDOM COME

And she obtained grace and favor in his sight. Esther 2:17
THE BOOKS OF
ESTHER & RUTH
BIBLE-BASED WORKBOOK
Take an adventure into the amazing Books of Esther and Ruth and test your knowledge as you go!
PROJECT KINGDOM COME

they brought Daniel and threw him into the lions' den. Daniel 6:16
THE BOOKS OF
DANIEL & JOB
BIBLE-BASED WORKBOOK
Take an adventure into the amazing Books of Daniel and Job and test your knowledge as you go!
PROJECT KINGDOM COME

Behold, a virgin shall be with child. Matthew 1:23
THE BOOK OF
MATTHEW
BIBLE-BASED WORKBOOK
Take an adventure into the amazing Book of Matthew and test your knowledge as you go!
PROJECT KINGDOM COME

Let us go into the next towns, that I may preach there also. Mark 1:38
THE BOOK OF
MARK
BIBLE-BASED WORKBOOK
Take an adventure into the amazing Book of Mark and test your knowledge as you go!
PROJECT KINGDOM COME

there they crucified Him. Luke 23:33
THE BOOK OF
LUKE
BIBLE-BASED WORKBOOK
Take an adventure into the amazing Book of Luke and test your knowledge as you go!
PROJECT KINGDOM COME

I am the resurrection and the life. John 11:25
THE BOOK OF
JOHN
BIBLE-BASED WORKBOOK
Take an adventure into the amazing Book of John and test your knowledge as you go!
PROJECT KINGDOM COME

In the name of Jesus Christ of Nazareth, rise up and walk. Acts 3:6
THE BOOK OF
ACTS
BIBLE-BASED WORKBOOK
Take an adventure into the amazing Book of Acts and test your knowledge as you go!
PROJECT KINGDOM COME

Look, He is coming with the clouds, and every eye will see Him. Revelation 1:7
THE BOOK OF
REVELATION
BIBLE-BASED WORKBOOK
Take an adventure into the amazing Book of Revelation and test your knowledge as you go!
PROJECT KINGDOM COME

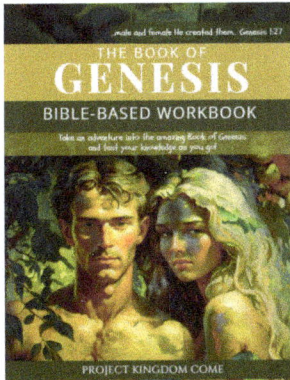

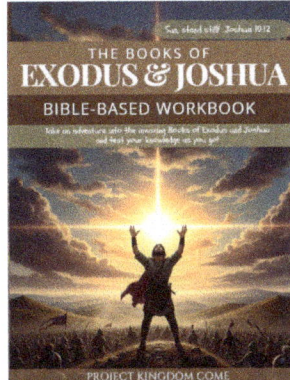

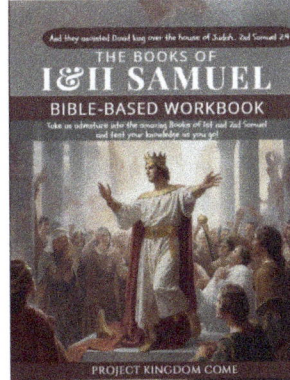

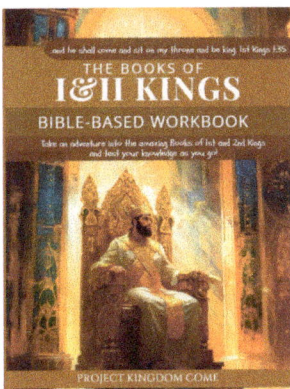

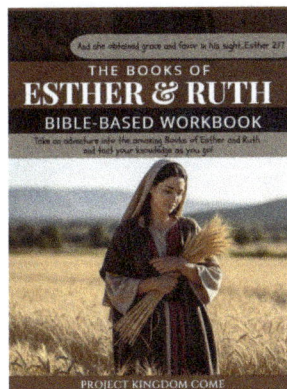

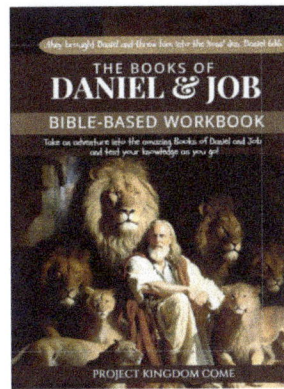

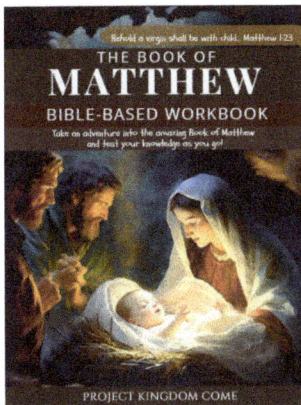

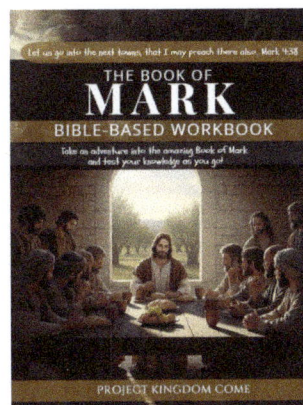

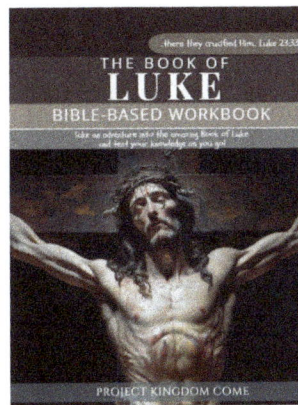

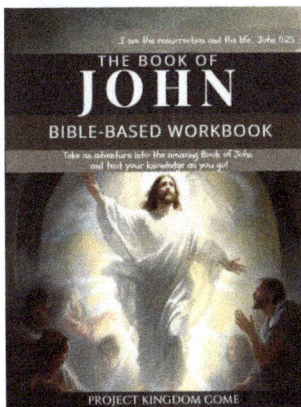

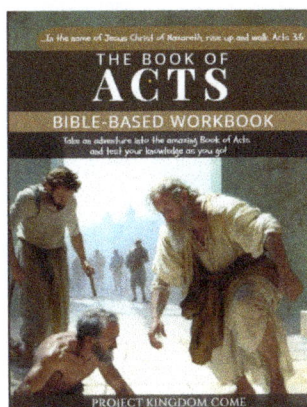

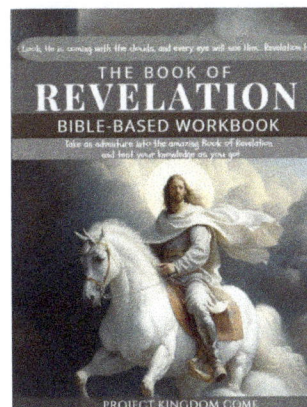

WWW.MYBIBLEWORKBOOKS.COM

PROJECT KINGDOM COME
Sword of the Word

This workbook belongs to:

_____

_____

_____

Leave your mark!

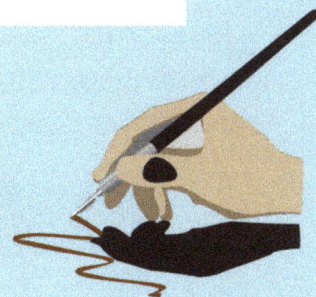

HOW TO USE THIS WORKBOOK

This workbook is designed to help young people explore the treasures in God's Word while having fun, growing in faith, and learning how to search the Scriptures for life's answers.

Here is what you will find inside:

Multiple Choice Questions — Each question comes directly from Scripture and includes a reference verse to help with locating the answer in the Bible. If possible, use a physical Bible to search for the answers.

Weekly Segments — Questions are grouped in weekly categories that could also be completed in a shorter or longer time frame.

Weekly Memory Verses — At the start of every week is a Bible verse to memorize. Each day of that week will repeat that memory verse with a chance to test memorization at the end of the week.

Certificate of Completion — At the end of the workbook, please find a Certificate of Achievement, ready for the child's name and parent or teacher's signature. Celebrate the accomplishment of studying an entire book in the Bible!

Answer Key — The workbook contains an answer key to serve as a support tool for parents or teachers reviewing the responses.

Recommendation for Parents and/or Teachers: Review the responses with your child or student and discuss lessons learned or interesting insights, to improve the child's retention and enrichment in the knowledge of God's word.

You can do all things through Christ who gives you strength!
Philippians 4:13

SAMPLE QUESTION...

HOW TO USE THIS WORKBOOK

Reading the reference verse will always lead you to the correct answer!

In the beginning was: (John 1:1)

A The Word
B. Heaven and Earth
C. Heaven only
D. Earth only

The number that comes after the book is the 'Chapter'

This is the name of a book in the Bible

John 1:1

The number after the chapter is the 'Verse'

NOW TEST YOURSELF! FIND JOSHUA CHAPTER 1 VERSE 8 IN YOUR BIBLE!

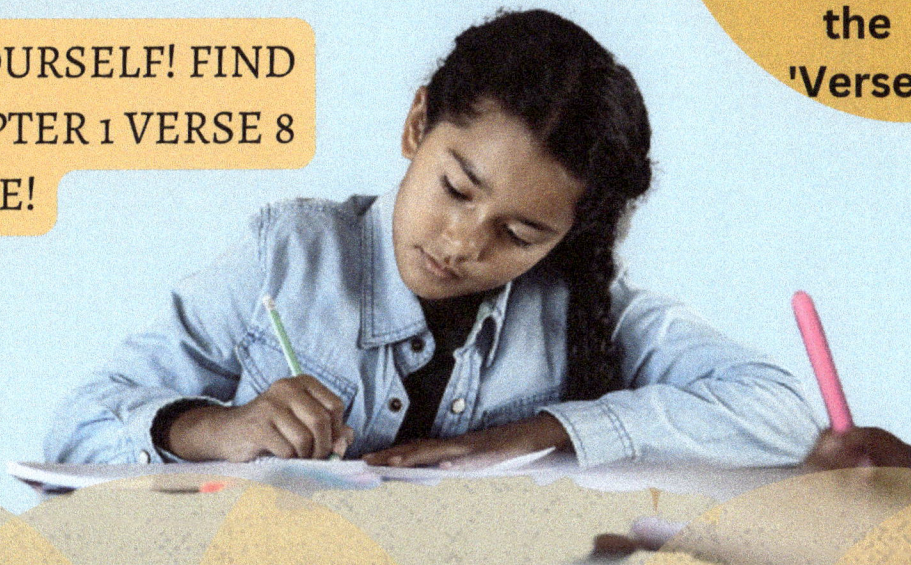

INTRODUCTION: THE BOOK OF LUKE

The Savior for Everyone

The **Book of Luke** is a beautifully detailed and compassionate account of the life, ministry, death, and resurrection of Jesus Christ. Written by **Luke, a physician and close companion of Paul,** this Gospel was carefully researched and written so that we may know the certainty of what we believe.

Luke highlights Jesus as the **perfect Son of Man** who came to seek and save the lost. More than any other Gospel, **Luke shows Jesus reaching out to those often forgotten by society:** women, children, the poor, the sick, and the outcast. This book reminds us that the Gospel is for everyone, no matter their background, status, or story.

Through stories like the **Good Samaritan** and the **Prodigal Son,** Luke reveals the heart of God as compassionate, merciful, and full of grace. He also gives us the longest and most detailed look into Jesus' birth, as well as powerful parables, healings, and teachings.

As you go through this workbook, you will discover:
- **How Jesus lived with perfect love, humility, and obedience**
- **The parables that reveal God's heart for the lost and broken**
- **The bold truth that Jesus is the Savior of all people**
- **The power of prayer, faith, and the Holy Spirit**

As you walk through the pages of Luke, you'll come face-to-face with the kindness of Jesus, the power of His words, and the depth of His sacrifice.

Let every chapter strengthen your faith and draw you closer to the One who came to rescue us all.

"For the Son of Man has come to seek and to save that which was lost." — Luke 19:10

WEEK 1

1. Who was the book of Luke written to? (Luke 1:3)

A. Timothy
B. Theo
C. Theophilus
D. Thessalonians

2. What is the name of Zacharias' wife? (Luke 1:5)

A. Esther
B. Edna
C. Elizabeth
D. Emily

3. What was Zechariah's role in serving God? (Luke 1:5)

A. A worship leader
B. An usher
C. A priest
D. A temple helper

WEEK 1 MEMORY VERSE: LUKE 1:37
For with God nothing will be impossible.

**4. What does the Bible say about Zechariah and Elizabeth?
(Luke 1:6)**

A. They were faithful pastors
B. They were righteous and lived blamelessly
C. They were wealthy and respected
D. They were popular Bible teachers

**5. What did Zechariah and Elizabeth long for, even in their old age?
(Luke 1:7)**

A. Wisdom
B. Wealth
C. A child
D. A bigger home

6. Where was Zacharias when the angel appeared to him? (Luke 1:11)

A. At home
B. In the temple, near the altar of incense
C. Sleeping in bed
D. Walking in the fields

WEEK 1 MEMORY VERSE: LUKE 1:37
For with God nothing will be impossible.

7. What did the angel say about Zechariah's prayers? (Luke 1:13)

A. God was sending him great riches
B. God was proud of his service
C. God had heard him and would give him a son
D. That he would serve as high priest

8. What name did the angel tell Zechariah to give his son? (Luke 1:13)

A. Jonah
B. John
C. Jeremiah
D. Jeremy

9. What was Zechariah's son not allowed to drink? (Luke 1:15)

A. Goat milk
B. Wine or strong drink
C. Beet juice
D. Water from the river

WEEK 1 MEMORY VERSE: LUKE 1:37
For with God nothing will be impossible.

10. What would fill Zechariah's son even before he was born? (Luke 1:15)

A. Strength
B. Discernment
C. The Holy Spirit
D. Wisdom

11. Which prophet's spirit and power would be upon Zechariah's son? (Luke 1:17)

A. Elisha
B. Elijah
C. Isaiah
D. Micah

12. What was John's God-given mission? (Luke 1:16–17)

A. To turn the children of Israel to the Lord their God.
B. To turn the hearts of the fathers to the children and the disobedient to the wisdom of the just
C. To prepare the people for the coming of the Lord
D. All the above

13. Why did Zacharias doubt the angel's message? (Luke 1:18)

A. He thought angels weren't real
B. He believed he and Elizabeth were too old to have a child
C. He was dreaming
D. He only doubted a part of the message

14. What is the name of the angel God sent to Zacharias? (Luke 1:19)

A. Moses
B. Gabriel
C. Michael
D. Presence

15. What was the punishment for Zechariah's disbelief? (Luke 1:20)

A. He went blind
B. He couldn't speak
C. He became deaf
D. He became weak

WEEK 1 MEMORY VERSE: LUKE 1:37
For with God nothing will be impossible.

WEEK 1

16. How long did Elizabeth stay hidden after she became pregnant? (Luke 1:24)

A. Three months
B. Five months
C. Two months
D. Four months

17. What was the name of the young virgin in Nazareth engaged to Joseph? (Luke 1:27)

A. Ruth
B. Mary
C. Esther
D. Magdalene

18. Which angel was sent to visit Mary? (Luke 1:26)

A. Elijah
B. Moses
C. Gabriel
D. Michael

WEEK 1 MEMORY VERSE: LUKE 1:37
For with God nothing will be impossible.

19. What name did the angel say Mary's Son would be called? (Luke 1:31)

A. Adonai

B. Jesus

C. Elohim

D. Emmanuel

20. In what way would Mary conceive? (Luke 1:35)

A. By the power of the Holy Spirit

B. By wind

C. By fire

D. By human wisdom

21. What does Luke 1:37 state?

A. It is well with my soul

B. If you believe, you will receive whatever you ask for in prayer

C. For with God, nothing will be impossible

D. What a mighty God we serve

WEEK 1 MEMORY VERSE: LUKE 1:37
For with God nothing will be impossible.

"
You are my hiding place and my shield; I hope in your word (Psalm 119:114)
"

Great job completing the week!

Did you memorize the daily verse?
Test yourself by writing it here...

_____

_____

_____

_____

_____

_____

Use this space to draw a scene from the Bible or reflect on something you learned, felt or experienced...

WEEK 2

22. What did Mary say in response to the angel's message? (Luke 1:38)

A. I am blessed to be a blessing
B. For with God, nothing will be impossible
C. Let it be to me according to your word
D. Your wish is my command

23. What is the relationship between Mary and Elizabeth? (Luke 1:36)

A. They are great friends
B. They are neighbors
C. They are relatives (Cousins)
D. They attended the same church

24. What happened to the baby in Elizabeth's womb when Mary greeted her? (Luke 1:44)

A. It kicked really hard
B. It leaped for joy
C. It worshiped
D. It started to hiccup

WEEK 2 MEMORY VERSE: LUKE 2:11
For there is born to you this day in the city of David a Savior, who is Christ the Lord.

WEEK 2

25. What happened 8 days after Zechariah's son was born? (Luke 1:58–59)

A. Neighbors came to bring gifts
B. The baby was circumcised
C. People offered sacrifices
D. A dedication service was held

26. What happened to Zechariah after he wrote the name "John"? (Luke 1:62–64)

A. He could walk again
B. He could see clearly
C. He could speak
D. He could hear

27. Where did John live before starting his ministry? (Luke 1:80)

A. In the temple
B. By the Jordan River
C. In the desert
D. In the city of Jerusalem

WEEK 2 MEMORY VERSE: LUKE 2:11

For there is born to you this day in the city of David a Savior, who is Christ the Lord.

WEEK 2

28. In which City was Jesus born? (Luke 2:4-7)

A. Nazareth
B. Galilee
C. Judea
D. Bethlehem

29. Where was baby Jesus laid after He was born? (Luke 2:7)

A. A manger
B. A chicken coop
C. The farm
D. The pulpit

30. Who were the first to hear about Jesus' birth from the angel? (Luke 2:8–11)

A. The shepherds
B. The wise men
C. Mary's family
D. Joseph's family

WEEK 2 MEMORY VERSE: LUKE 2:11
For there is born to you this day in the city of David a Savior,
who is Christ the Lord.

WEEK 2

31. What did Mary do after hearing all that was said about Jesus? (Luke 2:19)

A. She hid Him from danger
B. She kept those things in her heart and thought about them
C. She told everyone in town
D. She praised loudly in public

32. At what age was Jesus circumcised? (Luke 2:21)

A. Two days old
B. Eight days old
C. Fourteen years old
D. Seven days old

33. What was the name given to Mary's Son? (Luke 2:21)

A. Emmanuel
B. Jesus
C. Elohim
D. Adonai

WEEK 2 MEMORY VERSE: LUKE 2:11
For there is born to you this day in the city of David a Savior,
who is Christ the Lord.

34. What does the Law of Moses say about every firstborn male? (Luke 2:23)

A. He must be called holy to the Lord
B. He must be circumcised on the 7th day
C. He must offer prayers
D. All the above

35. What offering did Mary and Joseph give for Jesus, according to the law? (Luke 2:24)

A. Three newborn goats
B. A pair of turtle doves or two young pigeons
C. A lamb and a goat
D. A basket of grain

36. What was the name of the man who was promised he would not die before seeing the Messiah? (Luke 2:25–26)

A. Simeon
B. Simon
C. Peter
D. Theophilus

WEEK 2 MEMORY VERSE: LUKE 2:11
For there is born to you this day in the city of David a Savior, who is Christ the Lord.

WEEK 2

37. What was the name of the widow who worshiped God with fasting and prayer at the temple? (Luke 2:36)

A. Deborah
B. Peninnah
C. Prophetess Anna
D. Asher

38. How old was the widow who served God as she waited for the Messiah? (Luke 2:37)

A. 84 years old
B. 77 years
C. 88 years
D. 80 years

39. How old was Jesus when He stayed behind at the temple and talked with the teachers? (Luke 2:41–46)

A. Seven years old
B. Twelve years old
C. Fourteen years old
D. Seventeen years old

WEEK 2 MEMORY VERSE: LUKE 2:11
For there is born to you this day in the city of David a Savior, who is Christ the Lord.

WEEK 2

40. What does Luke 2:52 say about Jesus? (Luke 2:52)

A. Jesus increased in wisdom and stature, and in favor with God and men
B. Jesus grew tall and mighty
C. Jesus gained knowledge and riches
D. Jesus impressed the teachers at the temple

41. John warned the people to bear fruit worthy of repentance and not do what? (Luke 3:8)

A. Say to themselves they have Abraham as their Father (they are members of God's family through Abraham)
B. Say to themselves, they know Abraham
C. Say to themselves, they will do as Abraham did
D. Say to themselves that baptism is all that is required

42. What did John warn happens to every tree that does not bear good fruit? (Luke 3:9)

A. It is cut down and thrown into the fire
B. It is destroyed
C. It is excommunicated
D. It is chastised

WEEK 2 MEMORY VERSE: LUKE 2:11
For there is born to you this day in the city of David a Savior, who is Christ the Lord.

> "For you, O Lord, are my hope, my trust, O Lord, from my youth (Psalm 71:5)

Great job completing the week!

**Did you memorize the daily verse?
Test yourself by writing it here...**

**Use this space to draw a scene from the Bible or reflect
on something you learned, felt or experienced...**

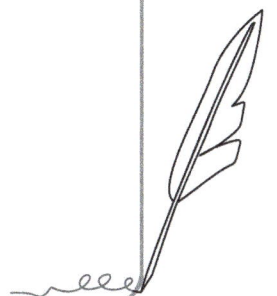

43. What advice did John give to the tax collectors? (Luke 3:12-13)

A. Forgive your debtors
B. Give to the poor
C. Do not collect more than what is required
D. Give to Caesar what belongs to Caesar

44. What advice did John give to the soldiers? (Luke 3:14)

A. Be kind and merciful
B. Don't intimidate or accuse anyone falsely, and be content with your wages
C. Serve with integrity
D. Rule with compassion

45. John said he baptized with water, but what would Jesus baptize with? (Luke 3:15–16)

A. Oil
B. The Holy Spirit and fire
C. Water
D. Prayers

WEEK 3 MEMORY VERSE: LUKE 6:31
And just as you want men to do to you, you also do to them likewise.

WEEK 3

46. What did John say he was unworthy to do for Jesus? (Luke 3:16)

A. Shake His hand
B. Eat with Him
C. Kiss Him
D. Untie the straps of His sandals

47. What will Jesus do with the wheat and the chaff? (Luke 3:17)

A. Gather the chaff and burn the wheat
B. Burn both together
C. Gather the wheat and burn the chaff
D. Store them all together

48. Who put John in prison and why? (Luke 3:19-20)

A. Caiaphas, for jealousy
B. Herod, because John rebuked him for marrying his brother's wife
C. Pilate, for stirring up trouble
D. Herod, because he was afraid of John's popularity

WEEK 3 MEMORY VERSE: LUKE 6:31
And just as you want men to do to you, you also do to them likewise.

WEEK 3

49. What happened when John baptized Jesus?
(Luke 3:21–22)

A. The Holy Spirit descended in bodily form upon him in the form of a dove
B. A voice from heaven said, "You are my beloved Son; in you, I am well pleased."
C. Both A and B
D. Jesus immediately began to heal the sick

50. How old was Jesus when He began His public ministry?
(Luke 3:23)

A. 17 years old
B. 21 years old
C. About 30 years old
D. 18 years old

51. How did Jesus respond when tempted to turn stones into bread?
(Luke 4:3–4)

A. You shall worship the Lord your God
B. You shall not tempt the Lord your God
C. Man shall not live by bread alone, but by every word of God
D. Jesus didn't respond

WEEK 3 MEMORY VERSE: LUKE 6:31
And just as you want men to do to you, you also do to them likewise.

WEEK 3

52. How did Jesus respond when tempted to throw Himself down from the temple? (Luke 4:5–8)

A. You shall not tempt the Lord your God
B. You shall worship the Lord your God
C. Man shall not live by bread alone
D. Jesus didn't answer

53. How did Jesus respond when offered all the kingdoms of the world? (Luke 4:9–12)

A. Man shall not live by bread alone
B. Get behind me, Satan! You shall worship the Lord your God and serve Him only
C. You shall not tempt the Lord your God
D. Jesus said nothing

54. Why did the people of Nazareth reject Jesus? (Luke 4:16-24)

A. They thought He was just Joseph's son
B. Jesus said no prophet is accepted in his hometown
C. Their hearts were hard
D. Both A and B

WEEK 3 MEMORY VERSE: LUKE 6:31
And just as you want men to do to you, you also do to them likewise.

WEEK 3

55. Why were the people amazed at Jesus' teaching? (Luke 4:31–32)

A. He taught them many new things
B. He taught in parables
C. His words had authority
D. He quoted other teachers

56. What did the unclean demon say about Jesus? (Luke 4:33–34)

A. You are Alpha and Omega
B. I know who You are—the Holy One of God
C. The demon said nothing
D. It is not by might but by the Spirit

57. What did the people say after Jesus cast out the unclean spirit? (Luke 4:33–36)

A. Jesus terrified demons
B. Jesus was not afraid
C. Jesus had authority and power, and the demons obeyed Him
D. Jesus was calm under pressure

WEEK 3 MEMORY VERSE: LUKE 6:31
And just as you want men to do to you, you also do to them likewise.

WEEK 3

58. Whose fever did Jesus heal at Simon Peter's house? (Luke 4:38–39)

A. Simon Peter's wife
B. His mother
C. His mother-in-law
D. His sister

59. Why did Jesus not allow the demons to speak when He cast them out? (Luke 4:40–41)

A. Because they hated Him
B. Because they were noisy
C. Because they knew He was the Christ
D. Because they begged Him

60. The people of Galilee begged Jesus not to leave them, but He refused to stay. Why? (Luke 4:42-43)

A. They didn't believe in Him
B. The Pharisees were coming for Him
C. He was sent to preach the Kingdom of God in other cities, too
D. He needed to do new things daily

WEEK 3 MEMORY VERSE: LUKE 6:31
And just as you want men to do to you, you also do to them likewise.

WEEK 3

61. What did Simon say when Jesus told him to cast the net into deep water? (Luke 5:4–5)

A. We already tried, and it didn't work

B. It's too late for fishing now

C. We toiled all night and caught nothing; nevertheless, at Your word, I will let down the net

D. Simon shrugged and walked away

62. After catching many fish, what did Simon say to Jesus? (Luke 5:6–8)

A. I'm sorry for doubting

B. Leave me, Lord, for I am a sinful man

C. You truly are the Son of God

D. Simon worshipped in silence

63. What was Jesus' response to Simon? (Luke 5:10)

A. I came to seek the lost

B. Your sins are forgiven

C. Do not be afraid. From now on you will catch men

D. I love you, Simon

WEEK 3 MEMORY VERSE: LUKE 6:31

And just as you want men to do to you, you also do to them likewise.

> **The Lord is my portion, therefore I will hope in him (Lamentations 3:24)**

Great job completing the week!

**Did you memorize the daily verse?
Test yourself by writing it here...**

_____

_____

_____

_____

_____

**Use this space to draw a scene from the Bible or reflect
on something you learned, felt or experienced...**

WEEK 4

**64. Who said, "Lord, if You are willing, You can make me clean"?
(Luke 5:12)**

A. A demon-possessed man
B. The woman with the issue of blood
C. A leper
D. Simon Peter

65. What was Jesus' response to "Lord, if you're willing, you can make me clean"? (Luke 5:12-13)

A. Get behind me, Satan!
B. Be healed
C. I am willing. Be cleansed
D. Go show the priest

66. What instructions did Jesus give to the man after healing him of leprosy? (Luke 5:14)

A. Bring a thanksgiving offering
B. Go to the temple and pray
C. Show yourself to the priest and offer a sacrifice as Moses commanded
D. Tell everyone what happened

WEEK 4 MEMORY VERSE: LUKE 6:45
Out of the abundance of the heart his mouth speaks.

WEEK 4

67. What did the men do to bring the paralyzed man to Jesus? (Luke 5:17–19)

A. They shouted to get Jesus' attention
B. They removed roof tiles and lowered him through the roof
C. They asked the disciples to help
D. They pushed through the crowd

68. Why did the scribes accuse Jesus of blasphemy when He forgave sins? (Luke 5:20–24)

A. Because He said He could forgive sins
B. Because He healed the man
C. Because He said He had power
D. Because He called Himself the Son of Man

69. What did Jesus say when asked why He ate with sinners and tax collectors? (Luke 5:29–32)

A. Those who are well have no need for a physician, but those who are sick do
B. I did not come to call the righteous but sinners to repentance
C. Both A and B
D. Jesus remained silent

WEEK 4 MEMORY VERSE: LUKE 6:45
Out of the abundance of the heart his mouth speaks.

WEEK 4

70. What was Jesus' response when asked why His disciples didn't fast? (Luke 5:33–35)

A. A day will come when the bridegroom will be taken from them; then they will fast
B. My disciples don't need to fast
C. They are not ready
D. Fasting isn't required anymore

71. Why did Jesus say no one puts new wine into old wineskins? (Luke 5:37)

A. Because wine gets better with age
B. Because the new wine will burst the old wineskins and spill
C. Because old wine tastes better
D. Because God's people should only drink from new wineskins

72. How did Jesus respond when the Pharisees complained about His disciples picking grain on the Sabbath? (Luke 6:1–5)

A. Jesus remained silent
B. David ate the showbread, and the Son of Man is Lord of the Sabbath
C. The Sabbath isn't important
D. The disciples were wrong

WEEK 4 MEMORY VERSE: LUKE 6:45
Out of the abundance of the heart his mouth speaks.

73. Why were the scribes and Pharisees watching Jesus closely at the synagogue? (Luke 6:6–11)

A. They were jealous
B. They wanted to see if He would heal on the Sabbath
C. They hoped to catch Him breaking the law
D. They were curious

74. How many disciples did Jesus choose? (Luke 6:13)

A. Seven
B. Ten
C. Three
D. Twelve

75. What name did Jesus give Simon? (Luke 6:14)

A. Peter
B. John
C. James
D. Sadon

WEEK 4 MEMORY VERSE: LUKE 6:45
Out of the abundance of the heart his mouth speaks.

WEEK 4

76. Which disciple became a traitor? (Luke 6:16)

A. Peter
B. Simon
C. Judas Iscariot
D. John

77. Blessed are you who are poor…. (Luke 6:20)

A. For your reward is great in heaven
B. For you shall be filled
C. For yours is the kingdom of God
D. For you shall laugh

78. Blessed are you who weep now… (Luke 6:21)

A. For your reward is great in heaven
B. For you shall be filled
C. For yours is the kingdom of God
D. For you shall laugh

WEEK 4 MEMORY VERSE: LUKE 6:45
Out of the abundance of the heart his mouth speaks.

WEEK 4

79. Blessed are you when people hate and insult you...
(Luke 6:22–23)

A. For your reward is great in heaven
B. For you shall be filled
C. For yours is the kingdom of God
D. For you shall laugh

80. Woe to you who are rich... (Luke 6:24)

A. For you have received your reward
B. For you shall hunger
C. For you shall mourn and weep
D. For you shall lose it all

81. Woe to you who are full now.. (Luke 6:25)

A. For you shall hunger
B. For so did their fathers to the false prophets
C. For you have received your consolation
D. For you shall mourn and weep

WEEK 4 MEMORY VERSE: LUKE 6:45
Out of the abundance of the heart his mouth speaks.

WEEK 4

82. Woe to you who laugh now.. (Luke 6:25)

A. For you shall hunger
B. For so did their fathers to the false prophets
C. For you have received your consolation
D. For you shall mourn and weep

83. Woe to you when all men speak well of you...(Luke 6:26)

A. For you shall hunger
B. For so did their fathers to the false prophets
C. For you have received your consolation
D. For you shall mourn and weep

84. Who does Jesus say we should love and do good to? (Luke 6:27)

A. All people
B. Your enemies and those who hate you
C. Everyone equally
D. Friends and neighbors

WEEK 4 MEMORY VERSE: LUKE 6:45
Out of the abundance of the heart his mouth speaks.

"

I am joyful in hope, patient in affliction, faithful in prayer (Romans 12:12)

"

Great job completing the week!

Did you memorize the daily verse?
Test yourself by writing it here...

_____

_____

_____

_____

_____

Use this space to draw a scene from the Bible or reflect
on something you learned, felt or experienced...

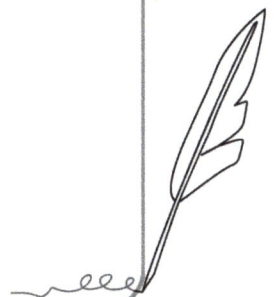

WEEK 5

85. What should you do to those who curse you? (Luke 6:28)

A. Forgive them
B. Pray for them
C. Bless them
D. Be still

86. What should you do to those who spitefully use you? (Luke 6:28)

A. Talk to them
B. Forgive them
C. Bless them
D. Pray for them

87. What should you do if someone takes your cloak? (Luke 6:29)

A. Give them your other cloak
B. Bless them
C. Forgive them
D. Do not withhold your tunic also

WEEK 5 MEMORY VERSE: LUKE 9:23
If anyone desires to come after Me, let him deny himself, and take up his cross daily, and follow Me.

WEEK 5

88. What should you do when someone takes what belongs to you? (Luke 6:30)

A. Don't demand it back
B. Show mercy
C. Take something from them
D. Ask them to return it

89. How should you treat others? (Luke 6:31)

A. With love
B. As you want them to treat you
C. As they treat you
D. With kindness

90. What more should you do besides loving those who love you? (Luke 6:32–35)

A. Love your enemies
B. Love your family
C. Honor all people
D. All the above

WEEK 5 MEMORY VERSE: LUKE 9:23
If anyone desires to come after Me, let him deny himself, and take up his cross daily, and follow Me.

WEEK 5

91. What should you do when you lend to others? (Luke 6:34–35)

A. Write and sign a promissory note
B. Lend hoping for nothing in return
C. Do not lend to friends
D. Do not lend to family members

92. Why should we be merciful? (Luke 6:36)

A. Because mercy conquers all
B. Because God is love
C. Because our Father is merciful
D. Because love never fails

93. Why should we not judge or condemn others? (Luke 6:37)

A. Because we are all sinners
B. So we will not be judged or condemned, and we will be forgiven
C. Because God sees everything
D. Because mercy wins

WEEK 5 MEMORY VERSE: LUKE 9:23
If anyone desires to come after Me, let him deny himself, and take up his cross daily, and follow Me.

94. What happens when you give? (Luke 6:38)

A. You will also receive

B. It will be returned to you, pressed down, shaken together, and running over

C. The same measure you give will be measured back to you

D. All the above

95. Why does Jesus say to remove the plank from your own eye first? (Luke 6:39–42)

A. In order to see clearly enough to help our brother remove the speck from their eye

B. Before we can see our brother's minor fault, we should first examine our own greater faults

C. We should not judge others before examining ourselves

D. All the above

96. What did Jesus teach about good and bad fruit? (Luke 6:43–45)

A. A tree is known by its fruit

B. Good trees produce good fruit, and bad trees produce bad fruit

C. Our words and actions come from what is in our hearts

D. All the above

WEEK 5 MEMORY VERSE: LUKE 9:23

If anyone desires to come after Me, let him deny himself, and take up his cross daily, and follow Me.

WEEK 5

97. What does Luke 6:45 say about the heart? (Luke 6:45)

A. Out of the heart, the spirit flows
B. Out of the heart, evil overflows
C. Out of the abundance of the heart, the mouth speaks
D. The heart speaks truth

98. What are those who hear and obey God's word compared to? (Luke 6:46–48)

A. The wisdom of Solomon
B. A house built on the rock
C. A man with great vision
D. A tree planted by water

99. What are those who hear but do not obey God's word compared to? (Luke 6:49)

A. A man who built their house on the earth without a foundation
B. A man whose house foundation collapsed because it could not withstand the storm
C. Both A and B
D. A man lost in darkness

WEEK 5 MEMORY VERSE: LUKE 9:23
If anyone desires to come after Me, let him deny himself, and take up his cross daily, and follow Me.

WEEK 5

100. Why did the centurion tell Jesus not to come to his house? (Luke 7:1–8)

A. He felt unworthy to have Jesus under his roof
B. He believed Jesus could heal by just speaking the word
C. He recognized Jesus' authority even from a distance
D. All the above

101. What did Jesus say about the centurion's faith? (Luke 7:9)

A. He had not seen such great faith, not even in Israel
B. Jesus was amazed by the centurion's love
C. Jesus admired the centurion's power
D. All the above

102. What happened when Jesus met the widow of Nain whose son had died? (Luke 7:11–17)

A. Jesus told her not to cry
B. Jesus raised her son back to life
C. The people were filled with awe and praised God
D. All the above

WEEK 5 MEMORY VERSE: LUKE 9:23
If anyone desires to come after Me, let him deny himself, and take up his cross daily, and follow Me.

WEEK 5

103. What did Jesus say when John the Baptist asked if He was the Messiah? (Luke 7:18–22)

A. Yes, I am
B. You will know the truth
C. Tell John what you've seen—the blind see, the lame walk, the lepers are cleansed
D. You will see greater things than these

104. What message did Jesus send to John? (Luke 7:23)

A. Blessed is he who comes in the name of the Lord
B. Blessed are those who wait on the Lord
C. Blessed is he who is not offended because of Me
D. Blessed are you when men persecute you

105. What did Jesus say about John the Baptist? (Luke 7:24–28)

A. He is more than a prophet
B. He was sent to prepare the way for Jesus
C. Among those born of women, none is greater than John—but the least in the kingdom is greater than he
D. All the above

WEEK 5 MEMORY VERSE: LUKE 9:23
If anyone desires to come after Me, let him deny himself, and take up his cross daily, and follow Me.

> **Surely there is a future, and my hope will not be cut off**
>
> (Proverbs 23:18)

Great job completing the week!

Did you memorize the daily verse?
Test yourself by writing it here...

_____

_____

_____

_____

_____

Use this space to draw a scene from the Bible or reflect
on something you learned, felt or experienced...

WEEK 6

106. What did people say about John and Jesus? (Luke 7:33–34)

A. John has a demon; Jesus is a glutton and friend of sinners
B. John is a loner; Jesus is fake
C. John fasts too much; Jesus doesn't fast enough
D. John is quiet; Jesus is too bold

107. What did Jesus say about the woman who poured perfume on His feet? (Luke 7:37–47)

A. He compared her to someone forgiven much who loves much
B. He said she was a good hostess
C. He called her righteous
D. Jesus did not say anything

108. Who had been healed by Jesus and delivered from seven demons? (Luke 8:2)

A. Joanna
B. Susanna
C. Mary Magdalene
D. Esther

WEEK 6 MEMORY VERSE: LUKE 10:27
You shall love the Lord your God with all your heart, with all your soul, with all your strength, and with all your mind, and your neighbor as yourself.

WEEK 6

109. Who were the women that supported Jesus' ministry? (Luke 8:1–3)

A. Joanna and Susanna
B. Mary Magdalene, Joanna, and Susanna
C. Esther, Joanna, and Mary
D. Joanna and Mary

110. In the parable of the sower, what happened to the seed that fell by the wayside? (Luke 8:5)

A. It sprang up and yielded a crop
B. It withered from a lack of moisture
C. It was trampled down and eaten by birds
D. It grew among thorns

111. What happened to the seed that fell on the rock? (Luke 8:6)

A. It was trampled
B. It was eaten by birds
C. It withered from a lack of moisture
D. It grew a little, then choked

WEEK 6 MEMORY VERSE: LUKE 10:27
You shall love the Lord your God with all your heart, with all your soul, with all your strength, and with all your mind, and your neighbor as yourself.

WEEK 6

112. What happened to the seed that fell among thorns? (Luke 8:7)

A. It grew and produced much fruit
B. It withered
C. It was eaten by birds
D. It was choked by the thorns

113. What happened to the seed that fell on good ground? (Luke 8:8)

A. It was trampled
B. It was choked
C. It produced a crop a hundredfold
D. It withered away

114. In the parable, what does the seed represent? (Luke 8:11)

A. Jesus
B. The Word of God
C. The Holy Spirit
D. Faith

WEEK 6 MEMORY VERSE: LUKE 10:27
You shall love the Lord your God with all your heart, with all your soul, with all your strength, and with all your mind, and your neighbor as yourself.

WEEK 6

115. What does the seed by the wayside mean? (Luke 8:12)

A. They hear, but the devil steals the word before they believe
B. They hear with joy but fall away in the time of temptation
C. They grow but get choked by the cares of the world
D. They bear fruit with patience

116. What does the seed on rocky soil mean? (Luke 8:13)

A. They hear with joy but have no root and fall away during temptation
B. They believe and bear fruit
C. They hear, but the devil steals the word
D. They are choked by riches

117. What does the seed among thorns mean? (Luke 8:14)

A. They hear but never believe
B. They are choked by cares, riches, and pleasures of life and bear no fruit
C. They fall during temptation
D. They bear fruit with patience

WEEK 6 MEMORY VERSE: LUKE 10:27
You shall love the Lord your God with all your heart, with all your soul, with all your strength, and with all your mind, and your neighbor as yourself.

WEEK 6

118. What does the seed on good ground mean? (Luke 8:15)

A. They fall away during temptation
B. They keep the word and bear fruit with patience
C. They hear and forget
D. They are choked by riches

119. Why should we put a lamp on a lampstand? (Luke 8:16–17)

A. So everyone can see the light
B. Because everything hidden will be revealed
C. So what's secret will come to light
D. All the above

120. What did Jesus ask His disciples after calming the storm? (Luke 8:23–25)

A. Where is your faith?
B. Why are you afraid?
C. Where is your power?
D. What did I teach you?

WEEK 6 MEMORY VERSE: LUKE 10:27
You shall love the Lord your God with all your heart, with all your soul, with all your strength, and with all your mind, and your neighbor as yourself.

WEEK 6

121. What did the name "Legion" mean? (Luke 8:30)

A. They were many
B. They came from a place called Legion
C. They were legendary
D. They came from the tombs

122. When the healed man from the Gadarenes begged to follow Jesus, what did Jesus say? (Luke 8:38–39)

A. You are not ready to follow Me
B. Go home and tell your family the great things God has done for you
C. Sell everything and follow Me
D. Go and reconcile with your friends

123. What was Jesus' response when He heard Jairus' daughter had died? (Luke 8:49–50)

A. Do not weep, she is not dead but sleeping
B. Do not be afraid, only believe
C. Your faith will make her well
D. It is well

WEEK 6 MEMORY VERSE: LUKE 10:27
You shall love the Lord your God with all your heart, with all your soul, with all your strength, and with all your mind, and your neighbor as yourself.

WEEK 6

124. How old was Jairus' daughter? (Luke 8:42)

A. 10 years old
B. 12 years old
C. 7 years old
D. 11 years old

125. Which disciples did Jesus allow to go with Him into Jairus' house? (Luke 8:51)

A. Simon, Peter, and James
B. Peter, James, and John
C. Simon, Thomas, and Mark
D. Simon, Mark, and Matthew

126. Why did the crowd laugh at Jesus when He arrived at Jairus' house? (Luke 8:52–53)

A. Because Jesus said the girl was only sleeping
B. Because they hated Him
C. Because they thought He was lying
D. All the above

"When men say there is a casting down, I will say there is a lifting up (Job 22:29)"

Great job completing the week!

Did you memorize the daily verse?
Test yourself by writing it here...

_____

_____

_____

_____

_____

Use this space to draw a scene from the Bible or reflect on something you learned, felt or experienced...

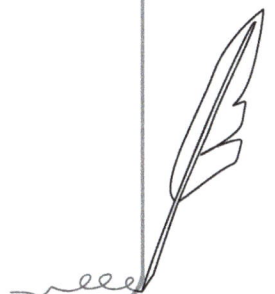

WEEK 7

127. Why did the woman with the issue of blood touch Jesus' garment? (Luke 8:43–47)

A. She thought it might get His attention
B. She believed if she touched the hem of His garment, she would be healed
C. She wanted Jesus to speak to her
D. She hoped to bring Him to her house

128. What did Jesus say to the woman with the issue of blood? (Luke 8:48)

A. Why did you touch Me?
B. Be healed of your affliction
C. Your faith has made you well; go in peace
D. I have not seen such great faith

129. What instructions did Jesus give the disciples when sending them out? (Luke 9:1–5)

A. Take nothing for the journey
B. Stay in the house where you are welcomed
C. Shake the dust off your feet if you are rejected
D. All the above

WEEK 7 MEMORY VERSE: LUKE 12:32
Do not fear, little flock, for it is your Father's good pleasure to give you the kingdom.

WEEK 7

130. How much food did the disciples have to feed the 5,000?
(Luke 9:11–14)

A. Two loaves and five fish
B. Two fish and five loaves
C. Twelve baskets of bread
D. Twelve baskets of fish

131. How much food was left over after feeding the multitudes?
(Luke 9:16–17)

A. Twelve baskets of fragments
B. Twelve baskets of bread
C. Seven baskets full
D. No food was left

132. Who correctly answered Jesus' question, "Who do you say I am?"
(Luke 9:18–20)

A. James said, "The Son of the Living God"
B. Matthew said, "The coming Messiah"
C. Simon Peter said, "You are the Christ of God"
D. Luke gave the right answer

WEEK 7 MEMORY VERSE: LUKE 12:32
Do not fear, little flock, for it is your Father's good pleasure to give you the kingdom.

WEEK 7

133. What did Jesus say would happen to Him? (Luke 9:21–22)

A. He might suffer and die
B. He would be rejected, killed, and raised on the third day
C. He would be killed by the Romans
D. He would be handed over to Pilate

134. Which of the following statements were made by Jesus? (Luke 9:23-26)

A. Deny yourself, take up your cross daily, and follow Me
B. Whoever loses his life for My sake will save it
C. If you are ashamed of Me, I will be ashamed of you
D. All the above

135. Which disciple was NOT present at the transfiguration? (Luke 9:28)

A. Peter
B. James
C. John
D. Matthew

WEEK 7 MEMORY VERSE: LUKE 12:32
Do not fear, little flock, for it is your Father's good pleasure to give you the kingdom.

WEEK 7

136. What happened during Jesus' transfiguration? (Luke 9:28–35)

A. Moses and Elijah appeared
B. A voice said, "This is My beloved Son. Hear Him!"
C. Jesus' face changed, and His robe became bright
D. All the above

137. What did Jesus say when His disciples couldn't cast out a demon? (Luke 9:37–42)

A. You are faithless and perverse
B. How long must I be with you?
C. He rebuked the demon and healed the boy
D. All the above

138. What did Jesus say when the disciples argued about who was greatest? (Luke 9:46–48)

A. Whoever receives this child in My name receives Me
B. Whoever receives Me receives the One who sent Me
C. He who is least among you is the greatest
D. All the above

WEEK 7 MEMORY VERSE: LUKE 12:32
Do not fear, little flock, for it is your Father's good pleasure to give you the kingdom.

WEEK 7

139. What did Jesus say when His disciples stopped someone from casting out demons in His name? (Luke 9:49–50)

A. Do not stop him—whoever is not against you is for you
B. Good job stopping him
C. You were right to protect My name
D. He will follow later

140. What did the disciples suggest when the Samaritan village rejected Jesus? (Luke 9:51–54)

A. The disciples asked Jesus if He would curse the town
B. The disciples asked Jesus if they should command fire to come down from heaven and consume the people as in the days of Elijah
C. The disciples asked Jesus to have mercy on the people
D. The disciples did not make any suggestions

141. When the people of the Samaritan village rejected Jesus, what did He say to His disciples who wanted to call down fire? (Luke 9:54–56)

A. The Son of Man did not come to destroy lives but to save them
B. Shake off the dust as a testimony
C. He was grieved by their rejection
D. He remembered the good Samaritan

WEEK 7 MEMORY VERSE: LUKE 12:32
Do not fear, little flock, for it is your Father's good pleasure to give you the kingdom.

WEEK 7

142. What was Jesus' response to the man who said, "I will follow You wherever You go"? (Luke 9:57–58)

A. You must take up your cross
B. Follow Me, and I'll make you a fisher of men
C. Foxes have holes, birds have nests, but the Son of Man has nowhere to lay His head
D. I am the way, the truth, and the life

143. What did Jesus say to the man who wanted to bury his father before following Him? (Luke 9:59–60)

A. Let the dead bury their own dead; you go preach the Kingdom of God
B. You must first deny yourself
C. No one comes to the Father except through Me
D. Forget about yourself first

144. Which of these is NOT part of Jesus' instructions to the seventy? (Luke 10:1–6)

A. Pray for more laborers
B. Don't carry a money bag or greet anyone on the road
C. Be strong and courageous
D. Speak peace to the homes you enter

WEEK 7 MEMORY VERSE: LUKE 12:32
Do not fear, little flock, for it is your Father's good pleasure to give you the kingdom.

WEEK 7

145. What instructions did Jesus give regarding how to treat cities and homes? (Luke 10:7–11)

A. Heal the sick and say, "The Kingdom of God has come near"
B. Eat and drink what the people provide
C. Shake the dust off your feet if you are not received
D. All the above

146. Jesus gave His disciples authority to trample over all of the following except _____ (Luke 10:19)

A. Serpents
B. Scorpions
C. All the powers of the enemy
D. Holy Fire

147. What did Jesus say the disciples should rejoice about most? (Luke 10:20)

A. That they had power over demons
B. That nothing could hurt them
C. That Satan fell like lightning
D. That their names are written in heaven

WEEK 7 MEMORY VERSE: LUKE 12:32
Do not fear, little flock, for it is your Father's good pleasure to give you the kingdom.

> "I shall not die, but live, and declare the works of the Lord in the land of the living
> (Psalm 118:17)"

Great job completing the week!

Did you memorize the daily verse?
Test yourself by writing it here...

_____

_____

_____

_____

_____

_____

Use this space to draw a scene from the Bible or reflect on something you learned, felt or experienced...

WEEK 8

148. Jesus said that no one knows the Father except the son. Who else knows the Father? (Luke 10:22)

A. All people
B. Those to whom the Son chooses to reveal Him
C. The chosen ones
D. The prophets

149. What is written in the law about inheriting eternal life? (Luke 10:25–27)

A. Love the Lord your God with all your heart, soul, strength, and mind
B. Love your neighbor as yourself
C. Keep the Sabbath Day holy
D. Both A & B

150. In the parable of the good Samaritan, which of the men was a good neighbor? (Luke 10:30-36)

A. The Levite
B. The Priest
C. The Good Samaritan
D. None of them

WEEK 8 MEMORY VERSE: LUKE 15:7
I say to you that likewise there will be more joy in heaven over one sinner who repents than over ninety-nine just persons who need no repentance.

WEEK 8

151. Which of the two sisters was doing all the work when Jesus visited their home? (Luke 10:38-40)

A. Mary
B. Martha
C. Magdalene
D. Marra

152. What was Jesus' response when one of the sisters complained that the other sister was not being helpful? (Luke 10:41-42)

A. Mary has chosen what is better, and it won't be taken away from her
B. Martha, stop complaining
C. Mary, help your sister
D. He remained silent

153. Which of the following lines are part of the Lord's Prayer? (Luke 11:1–4)

A. Hallowed be Your name
B. Give us this day our daily bread
C. Lead us not into temptation
D. All the above

WEEK 8 MEMORY VERSE: LUKE 15:7
I say to you that likewise there will be more joy in heaven over one sinner who repents than over ninety-nine just persons who need no repentance.

WEEK 8

154. What does the parable of the friend who comes at midnight teach us? (Luke 11:5-8)

A. The importance of prayer
B. The power of faith
C. The power of persistence in prayer
D. The mystery of the midnight hour

155. How did Jesus illustrate that God gives good gifts to those who ask? (Luke 11:9–13)

A. No father gives a stone when a child asks for bread
B. No father gives a serpent when asked for a fish
C. If earthly fathers give good gifts, how much more your Heavenly Father
D. All the above

156. What did the Pharisees accuse Jesus of after He cast out a mute demon? (Luke 11:14–15)

A. Being a fake prophet
B. Using the power of Beelzebub to cast out demons
C. Blaspheming
D. Healing on the Sabbath

WEEK 8 MEMORY VERSE: LUKE 15:7
I say to you that likewise there will be more joy in heaven over one sinner who repents than over ninety-nine just persons who need no repentance.

WEEK 8

157. What was Jesus' response to being accused of casting out demons by Beelzebub? (Luke 11:17–20)

A. A house divided cannot stand
B. If I cast out demons by the finger of God, the Kingdom of God has come
C. He remained silent
D. Both A & B

158. What happens when a stronger man overtakes the one guarding a palace? (Luke 11:21–22)

A. He overcomes him
B. He takes his armor
C. He divides the spoils
D. All the above

159. Jesus said, "He who is not with Me..." (Luke 11:23)

A. Is not worthy
B. Is against Me, and he who does not gather with Me scatters
C. Will be rejected
D. Scatters in vain

WEEK 8 MEMORY VERSE: LUKE 15:7
I say to you that likewise there will be more joy in heaven over one sinner who repents than over ninety-nine just persons who need no repentance.

160. What did Jesus teach about unclean spirits? (Luke 11:24-26)

A. They go through dry places seeking rest but find none, so they return to the house from which they came

B. When they return to their original house and find it empty, they look for seven other spirits more wicked than them

C. They reenter the original house and dwell there, and the state of that man is worse than it was before

D. All the above

161. What did Jesus say when a woman shouted, "Blessed is the womb that bore You"? (Luke 11:27–28)

A. Blessed are you among women, and blessed is the fruit of your womb

B. Shalom, Shalom!

C. May peace be with you, my peace I give to you

D. More than that, blessed are those who hear the word of God and keep it

162. Why did Jesus say no sign would be given except the sign of Jonah? (Luke 11:29–32)

A. At the preaching of Jonah, the people of Nineveh repented but one who is greater than Jonah was here, and they had refused to repent

B. The Queen of the South travelled far to hear the wisdom of Solomon but one greater than Solomon was here, and they had refused to listen

C. As Jonah became a sign to the Ninevites, the Son of Man will also be to this generation.

D. All the above

WEEK 8 MEMORY VERSE: LUKE 15:7

I say to you that likewise there will be more joy in heaven over one sinner who repents than over ninety-nine just persons who need no repentance.

WEEK 8

163. In Luke 11:34, Jesus likens the eye to _____

A. A candle
B. A fire
C. The lamp of the body
D. The light of the world

164. What did Jesus say to the Pharisees who focused on outer cleanliness but were full of greed inside? (Luke 11:37–41)

A. Give generously to the poor, and your heart will be clean
B. Use hyssop to purify yourselves
C. Eat only what is acceptable
D. Focus on external holiness

165. Why did Jesus warn the Pharisees about their hypocrisy? (Luke 11:42)

A. They tithed faithfully but ignored justice and the love of God
B. They were too proud
C. They lacked gentleness
D. They broke the Sabbath

WEEK 8 MEMORY VERSE: LUKE 15:7
I say to you that likewise there will be more joy in heaven over one sinner who repents than over ninety-nine just persons who need no repentance.

WEEK 8

166. Which of these was NOT a caution Jesus gave to religious leaders? (Luke 11:43–46)

A. They loved the best seats in the synagogues and respectful greetings as they walked in the marketplaces
B. They loaded men with unbearable religious demands
C. They did not help ease the burdens they inflicted on the people
D. They paid attention to religious law

167. Why did Jesus rebuke the lawyers/experts in religious law? (Luke 11:52)

A. Because they took away the key of knowledge from the people
B. Because they did not enter the Kingdom of God
C. Because they prevented others from entering the Kingdom of God
D. All the above

168. What did Jesus mean by "the leaven of the Pharisees"? (Luke 12:1)

A. Their bread
B. Their food
C. Their hypocrisy
D. All the above

WEEK 8 MEMORY VERSE: LUKE 15:7
I say to you that likewise there will be more joy in heaven over one sinner who repents than over ninety-nine just persons who need no repentance.

"

Jesus came that I may have life and have it more abundantly (John 10:10)

"

Great job completing the week!

Did you memorize the daily verse?
Test yourself by writing it here...

_____

_____

_____

_____

_____

_____

Use this space to draw a scene from the Bible or reflect
on something you learned, felt or experienced...

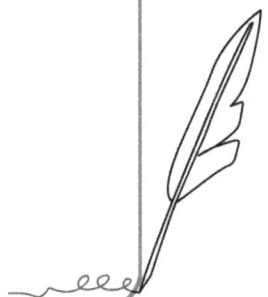

169. Why did Jesus tell His disciples not to fear? (Luke 12:4–7)

A. People can only harm the body, not the soul
B. They are worth more than many sparrows
C. God knows the number of hairs on their heads
D. All the above

170. Why should we confess Jesus before people? (Luke 12:8-9)

A. So He will confess us before the angels
B. Because if we deny Him, He will deny us
C. Because we love Him
D. Both A and B

171. Which sin did Jesus say will not be forgiven? (Luke 12:10)

A. Blasphemy against the Son
B. Blasphemy against the Holy Spirit
C. Blasphemy against the Father
D. Blasphemy against the angels

WEEK 9 MEMORY VERSE: LUKE 18:27
The things which are impossible with men are possible with God.

WEEK 9

172. What did Jesus say His disciples should do when they are brought before rulers? (Luke 12:11–12)

A. Stay silent
B. Speak boldly and quickly
C. The Holy Spirit will teach them what to say
D. Be strong and courageous

173. What's the lesson from the parable of the rich fool? (Luke 12:13–21)

A. That we should not lay up treasure on earth and not be rich toward God
B. Life is short, be sure to be rich in heavenly treasure
C. It is foolish to store up earthly wealth but not have a rich relationship with God
D. All the above

174. Why did Jesus say not to worry? (Luke 12:22–28)

A. God feeds the birds, and we are worth more than birds
B. God clothes the lilies, and we are of more valuable
C. Worry cannot add anything to our lives
D. All the above

WEEK 9 MEMORY VERSE: LUKE 18:27
The things which are impossible with men are possible with God.

WEEK 9

175. Instead of worrying, what should we focus on? (Luke 12:29–31)

A. Getting to heaven
B. Reading the Bible
C. Seeking first the Kingdom of God
D. Being righteous

176. What benefit comes from giving to those in need? (Luke 12:32–33)

A. It feels good
B. It stores treasure in heaven that cannot be stolen
C. God will reward you with more riches
D. You'll be blessed with peace

177. Jesus said that "where your treasure is.........." (Luke 12:34)

A. There, your heart will also be
B. It is recorded in heaven
C. God marks it in heaven
D. All the above

WEEK 9 MEMORY VERSE: LUKE 18:27
The things which are impossible with men are possible with God.

WEEK 9

178. What does Jesus teach in the parable of the faithful and evil servant? (Luke 12:35–40)

A. Be ready for the Lord's return
B. Blessed is the servant found watching
C. The Lord will return at an unexpected hour
D. All the above

179. Who is the good and faithful servant? (Luke 12:42–48)

A. One who manages well what the master gives
B. One who does the master's will
C. One who stays faithful even when the master delays
D. All the above

180. What did Jesus teach about responsibility and accountability? (Luke 12:48)

A. To whom much is given, much will be required; and to whom much has been entrusted, even more will be asked
B. To whom much is given, much will be received
C. To whom much is committed, everything will be taken
D. To whom little is given, much is expected

WEEK 9 MEMORY VERSE: LUKE 18:27
The things which are impossible with men are possible with God.

181. Jesus said He did not come to bring peace but division, meaning that family members will be split; those for and against Him (Luke 12:49-53)

A. True
B. False

182. In Luke 12:54-56, why did Jesus call them hypocrites?

A. Because they had burdensome religious demands
B. Because they preferred the best seats in the synagogues
C. Because they could read the signs of nature but not discern the spiritual times
D. Because they hated each other

183. "Agree with your adversary before he hands you over to the judge and you are thrown in prison." Is this true or false? (Luke 12:57–59)

A. False
B. True

WEEK 9 MEMORY VERSE: LUKE 18:27
The things which are impossible with men are possible with God.

WEEK 9

184. Jesus teaches that those who perish do not perish because they are worse sinners than those who did not perish. What does He caution the people to do? (Luke 13:1-5)

A. Say thank you
B. Repent of their sins
C. Run and hide
D. Try to be perfect

185. In the parable of the barren fig tree, why did the vineyard owner want it cut down? (Luke 13:6–9)

A. It was in the way
B. It had not borne fruit and was using up good soil
C. It didn't provide shade
D. There were too many trees already

186. How did Jesus respond to the synagogue ruler who was angry about healing on the Sabbath? (Luke 13:10–17)

A. He said they too worked on the Sabbath by watering their animals
B. He remained silent
C. He was also upset
D. He ignored them

WEEK 9 MEMORY VERSE: LUKE 18:27
The things which are impossible with men are possible with God.

WEEK 9

187. What does the mustard seed represent in Jesus' parable? (Luke 13:18–19)

A. A small but powerful tool
B. The few who enter heaven
C. The Kingdom of God growing from small beginnings to great impact
D. A seed that should not be ignored

188. In the parable of the leaven, what did Jesus teach about the Kingdom of God? (Luke 13:20–21)

A. It is vast
B. It is powerful and spreads through everything like yeast in dough
C. It is real
D. It is mighty

189. Why should we strive to enter through the narrow gate? (Luke 13:22-27)

A. Because a time is coming when the entrance door will be shut
B. Because evildoers will not be allowed in
C. Because some will be turned away by the Lord
D. All the above

WEEK 9 MEMORY VERSE: LUKE 18:27
The things which are impossible with men are possible with God.

> ## "
> ## I honor my Father and my Mother that my days may be long (Exodus 20:12)
> ## "

Great job completing the week!

**Did you memorize the daily verse?
Test yourself by writing it here...**

_____

_____

_____

_____

_____

_____

**Use this space to draw a scene from the Bible or reflect
on something you learned, felt or experienced...**

WEEK 10

190. "The last shall be first, and the first shall be last." Is this statement true? (Luke 13:30)

A. True
B. False

191. Which city did Jesus grieve over for killing God's prophets? (Luke 13:34)

A. Galilee
B. Jerusalem
C. Judea
D. Bethlehem

192. What did Jesus teach about choosing seats at a wedding feast? (Luke 14:7–11)

A. Don't take the seat of honor in case someone more important comes
B. Sit at the lowest place so you may be honored later
C. Those who humble themselves will be exalted
D. All the above

WEEK 10

193. Why should we invite the poor and disadvantaged to our feasts? (Luke 14:12–14)

A. Because God desires it
B. Because it shows mercy
C. Because though they can't repay, God will reward us
D. Because we are to feed the hungry

194. What does the parable of the great supper teach us? (Luke 14:16–24)

A. Guests who were initially invited will miss the feast and be replaced by outcasts and outsiders
B. Guests who were initially invited put their everyday business ahead of the great invite and therefore will miss the great supper
C. All the above
D. None of the above

195. What does Jesus say is the cost of being His disciple? (Luke 14:25–33)

A. Loving Him more than family and friends
B. Denying ourselves completely
C. Giving up everything for Him
D. All the above

WEEK 10 MEMORY VERSE: LUKE 19:10
For the Son of Man came to seek and to save the lost.

WEEK 10

196. What lesson is taught in the parable of the lost sheep? (Luke 15:1–7)

A. A good shepherd searches for the one lost sheep
B. A lost sheep represents a sinner
C. Heaven rejoices over one sinner who repents
D. All the above

197. In the parable of the lost coin, what does the coin represent? (Luke 15:8–10)

A. Talent
B. Wealth
C. Favor
D. A sinner

198. What had the prodigal son prepared to ask his Father upon his return? (Luke 15:17-19)

A. To become a better son
B. For another inheritance
C. To be treated like a hired servant
D. For a second chance

WEEK 10 MEMORY VERSE: LUKE 19:10
For the Son of Man came to seek and to save the lost.

WEEK 10

199. What did the father do when he saw his lost son returning? (Luke 15:20–23)

A. He ran to him, embraced him, and threw a feast for him
B. He gave him a second inheritance
C. He made him a servant
D. He turned him away

200. Why was the older brother upset with his Father? (Luke 15:25-30)

A. He was angry that his father welcomed his brother back
B. He didn't think his brother deserved his father's warm welcome
C. He felt his faithfulness had been overlooked
D. Both B and C

201. What was the father's response to the older son who was upset about the celebration for his younger brother? (Luke 15:31–32)

A. "All that I have is yours."
B. "It is right to celebrate, because your brother was dead and is alive again."
C. "I will hold another feast for you later."
D. Both A and B

WEEK 10 MEMORY VERSE: LUKE 19:10
For the Son of Man came to seek and to save the lost.

WEEK 10

202. What did the unjust steward do when he found out he was going to be fired? (Luke 16:1–7)

A. He began to prepare
B. He changed the debts people owed to his master
C. He made friends by lowering the debts they owed
D. All the above

203. Why did the master praise the steward, even though he had been dishonest? (Luke 16:8)

A. Because he was wise and made friends quickly using what he had
B. Because he was honest and faithful
C. Because he helped the poor with his master's money
D. Because he asked for forgiveness and changed his ways

204. If you are unfaithful with unrighteous mammon (worldly riches) .... (Luke 16:11)

A. "Who will give you more money?"
B. "Who will trust you with true riches?"
C. "How can you be trusted with small things?"
D. "How can you be trusted with big things?"

WEEK 10 MEMORY VERSE: LUKE 19:10
For the Son of Man came to seek and to save the lost.

WEEK 10

205. Jesus said you cannot serve two masters. Who are these two masters? (Luke 16:13)

A. God and people
B. God and the devil
C. God and mammon (money)
D. God and self

206. Jesus said it is easier for heaven and earth to pass away than ————— to fail (Luke 16:17)

A. A miracle failing
B. The kingdom passing away
C. The Word of God failing
D. Heaven and earth passing away

207. True or False: Jesus taught that marriage doesn't matter to God. (Luke 16:18)

A. True
B. False

WEEK 10 MEMORY VERSE: LUKE 19:10
For the Son of Man came to seek and to save the lost.

WEEK 10

208. When the rich man was in torment, what did he ask Abraham to do? (Luke 16:24)

A. To bring him to heaven
B. To send someone to pour water on him
C. To ask Lazarus to dip his finger in water and cool his tongue
D. To ask Lazarus to give him a drink

209. Why didn't Abraham grant the rich man's request to warn his family? (Luke 16:27–31)

A. Because the people in his Father's house had Moses and the prophets to warn them
B. Because if the people in his Father's house did not listen to Moses or the prophets, they wouldn't be persuaded even if someone rose from the dead
C. Both A and B
D. None of the above

210. What did Jesus say you should do if your brother sins against you and then repents? (Luke 17:3)

A. Forgive him
B. Rebuke him and walk away
C. Ask the elders to help you
D. Stay upset for a while

WEEK 10 MEMORY VERSE: LUKE 19:10
For the Son of Man came to seek and to save the lost.

"

The LORD has done great things for me therefore I am glad (Psalm 126:3)

"

Great job completing the week!

Did you memorize the daily verse?
Test yourself by writing it here...

_____

_____

_____

_____

_____

Use this space to draw a scene from the Bible or reflect on something you learned, felt or experienced...

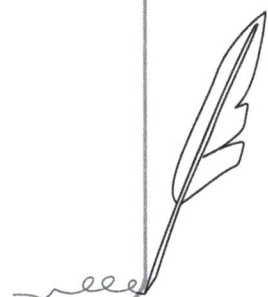

WEEK 11

211. If your brother keeps sinning against you and keeps asking for forgiveness, what should you do? (Luke 17:4)

A. Forgive him every time
B. Get help from your friends
C. Only forgive him once
D. Avoid him completely

212. How much faith did Jesus say could move a mulberry tree and cause it to be planted in the sea? (Luke 17:6)

A. A lot of faith in God and yourself
B. Faith, together with prayer and fasting
C. Faith as small as a mustard seed
D. Faith and good behavior

213. 213. What does the parable of the unworthy servants teach us? (Luke 17:7–10)

A. That we are only doing our duty when we obey God
B. That servants don't get rewards
C. That the greatest should be served first
D. That God only blesses those who are worthy

WEEK 11 MEMORY VERSE: LUKE 22:42
Nevertheless, not My will, but Yours, be done.

WEEK 11

214. How many of the ten lepers came back to thank Jesus after being healed? (Luke 17:11–19)

A. Ten
B. Seven
C. One
D. Five

215. What did Jesus say the coming of the Kingdom of God would be like? (Luke 17:20–36)

A. Like the days of Noah—people will be living normally, then suddenly judgment will come
B. Like the days of Lot—people will be eating and drinking, then destruction will come
C. It will be unexpected
D. All the above

216. What does the parable of the persistent widow teach us about prayer? (Luke 18:1–8)

A. We should always be persistent in prayer
B. Men ought always to pray and never give up
C. God answers prayers and will avenge His elect who cry out day and night to Him
D. All the above

WEEK 11 MEMORY VERSE: LUKE 22:42
Nevertheless, not My will, but Yours, be done.

WEEK 11

217. In the parable of the Pharisee and the tax collector, who was NOT right with God, and why? (Luke 18:9–14)

A. The Pharisee - He was a hypocrite
B. The Pharisee – He considered himself righteous and despised others
C. The Tax Collector – He stole money from the people of God
D. The Tax Collector – He overtaxed the people

218. Was the Pharisee justified before God in the parable? (Luke 18:9–14)

A. Yes, because he fasted twice a week
B. Yes, because he gave tithes
C. All the above
D. No, he was not justified

219. What did Jesus say when His disciples tried to stop people from bringing babies to Him? (Luke 18:15–17)

A. "Let the children come to Me. Don't stop them!"
B. "Pray for the little ones."
C. "Bless the children and their families."
D. "Cast their burdens onto Me."

WEEK 11 MEMORY VERSE: LUKE 22:42
Nevertheless, not My will, but Yours, be done.

WEEK 11

220. What did Jesus say the rich young ruler must do to have eternal life? (Luke 18:18-23)

A. Sell all he had
B. Follow Jesus
C. Give to the poor
D. Sell all he had and give it to the poor that he may have treasure in heaven then come and follow Jesus

221. What did Jesus say is easier than a rich person entering the Kingdom of God? (Luke 18:24–25)

A. To be born again
B. To be filled with the Holy Spirit
C. For a camel to go through the eye of a needle
D. To find a needle in a haystack

222. When the disciples asked, "Who then can be saved?" what was Jesus' response? (Luke 18:26–27)

A. The things which are impossible with men are possible with God
B. You can do all things through Christ that gives you strength
C. All things are possible if you believe
D. None of the above

WEEK 11 MEMORY VERSE: LUKE 22:42
Nevertheless, not My will, but Yours, be done.

WEEK 11

223. What reward did Jesus promise to those who leave everything to follow Him? (Luke 18:28–30)

A. They shall be celebrated
B. They shall be honored
C. They shall be repaid many times over in this life and will have eternal life
D. All the above

224. What was Zacchaeus' profession? (Luke 19:1–2)

A. He was a Tax Assessor
B. He was a Tax Collector
C. He was a Loan Officer
D. He was a Finance Officer

225. Why were people upset when Jesus dined with Zacchaeus? (Luke 19:1–7)

A. They complained that Jesus was eating with a sinner
B. They complained because Jesus did not rebuke him for stealing their money
C. They wanted Jesus to be with them instead
D. They wanted Jesus to continue teaching them the word of God

WEEK 11 MEMORY VERSE: LUKE 22:42
Nevertheless, not My will, but Yours, be done.

WEEK 11

226. What is the lesson in the parable of the ten servants and minas? (Luke 19:11-26)

A. Everyone who uses well what they have been given will be given more

B. When you give, it will come back to you, good measure, shaken together and running over

C. If you remain in God, you will bear much fruit

D. To him who is given, much is expected

227. What kind of animal did Jesus tell the disciples to bring Him before entering Jerusalem? (Luke 19:30)

A. A calf

B. A colt

C. A lion

D. A cow

228. When the owners of the animal asked why the disciples were untying it, what did they say? (Luke 19:33–34)

A. The Lord has need of it

B. It is more blessed to give than to receive

C. It is better to give than to receive

D. All the above

WEEK 11 MEMORY VERSE: LUKE 22:42
Nevertheless, not My will, but Yours, be done.

WEEK 11

229. What happened after the animal was brought to Jesus? (Luke 19:28–38)

A. The people threw their clothes on the colt, and Jesus sat on it
B. Many people spread their clothes on the road
C. The people cried out, saying, "Hosanna! Blessed is the King who comes in the name of the Lord! Peace in heaven and glory in the highest!
D. All the above

230. What did Jesus say when the Pharisees told Him to rebuke His disciples for praising Him? (Luke 19:39–40)

A. If they should keep silent, the stones would cry out
B. Jesus did not respond
C. Jesus called them hypocrites
D. If they should keep silent, the heavens would cry out

231. True or False: Jesus said, "My house shall be called a house of prayer, but you have made it a den of thieves." (Luke 19:45–46)

A. True
B. False

WEEK 11 MEMORY VERSE: LUKE 22:42
Nevertheless, not My will, but Yours, be done.

"

I do everything in love
(1 Corinthians 16:14)

"

Great job completing the week!

**Did you memorize the daily verse?
Test yourself by writing it here...**

_____

_____

_____

_____

_____

**Use this space to draw a scene from the Bible or reflect
on something you learned, felt or experienced...**

WEEK 12

232. Which scripture did Jesus say was fulfilled in the parable of the wicked vinedressers? (Luke 20:9–17)

A. The stone which the builders rejected has become the chief cornerstone
B. For I was hungry, and you didn't feed me
C. Give, and it will come back to you
D. I am the vine; you are the branches

233. How did Jesus explain that the Christ is more than just the Son of David? (Luke 20:41–44)

A. David himself said, "The Lord said to my Lord, sit at my right hand till I make your enemies your footstool"
B. If David calls Him Lord, how is He his Son?
C. Both A and B
D. Who do men say that I am?

234. Why did Jesus praise the widow who gave two small coins? (Luke 21:1–4)

A. Because she gave out of her poverty while others gave out of their abundance
B. Because she gave all that she had
C. Because she gave her whole livelihood
D. All the above

WEEK 12 MEMORY VERSE: LUKE 24:6
He is not here, but is risen!

WEEK 12

235. Which of the following is a sign of the end of the age?
(Luke 21:7-11)

A. Nation will rise against nation and kingdom against kingdom
B. There will be great earthquakes, famines, and pestilences
C. There will be wars and commotions
D. All the above are signs of the end of the age

236. What should believers do when facing persecution?
(Luke 21:12–19)

A. Don't worry about what to say, for God will give them wisdom
B. Know that they may be betrayed and hated, but not a hair on their head will be lost
C. Use the opportunity to testify for Jesus
D. All the above

237. Which of Jesus' disciples agreed to betray Him? (Luke 22:3-4)

A. James
B. Peter
C. Judas Iscariot
D. John

WEEK 12 MEMORY VERSE: LUKE 24:6
He is not here, but is risen!

WEEK 12

238. What did Jesus say when His disciples argued about who among them was the greatest? (Luke 22:24–27)

A. Whoever seeks first the kingdom of God
B. Whoever is last will be the greatest
C. Whoever is most willing will be the greatest
D. He who is greatest among you should be like the youngest, and the one who rules like one who serves

239. What is the name of the place where Jesus went to pray before being arrested? (Luke 22:39)

A. Gethsemane
B. Mount of Olives
C. Golgotha
D. Eden

240. What happened to Jesus as He prayed in agony before His arrest? (Luke 22:44)

A. His face glowed like the sun
B. His eyes glowed in the dark
C. His sweat became like great drops of blood falling down to the ground
D. His tears became like great drops of blood falling down to the ground

WEEK 12 MEMORY VERSE: LUKE 24:6
He is not here, but is risen!

WEEK 12

241. When Jesus returned from prayer, what were the disciples doing, and what did He say? (Luke 22:45–46)

A. Crying – Stop crying and pray
B. Sleeping – Why are you sleeping? Rise and pray so you won't fall into temptation
C. Praying – Why do you pray? The Son of Man must be taken
D. Plotting revenge – Vengeance is mine, says the Lord

242. What sign did Judas give the chief priests to show who Jesus was? (Luke 22:47)

A. A handshake
B. A kiss
C. A hug
D. Bowing

243. Why did Peter weep bitterly after the rooster crowed? (Luke 22:54-62)

A. Because he was sad to see Jesus arrested
B. Because he couldn't find the other disciples
C. Because he denied Jesus three times, just as Jesus had said
D. Because he felt helpless

WEEK 12 MEMORY VERSE: LUKE 24:6
He is not here, but is risen!

WEEK 12

244. Who was released instead of Jesus, and what had he done? (Luke 23:13–25)

A. Barabbas, a murderer
B. Barabbas, a thief
C. Beelzebub, a thief, and murderer
D. Bartholomew, a murderer

245. Who helped Jesus carry His cross? (Luke 23:26)

A. Peter
B. John
C. Simon of Cyrene
D. Matthew

246. What did Jesus say to the women who were weeping for Him? (Luke 23:27–30)

A. Do not weep for Me but for yourselves and your children.
B. The days are coming in which they will say, 'Blessed are the barren, wombs that never bore, and breasts which never nursed!'
C. The day is coming when they will begin 'to say to the mountains, "Fall on us!" and to the hills, "Cover us!
D. All the above

WEEK 12 MEMORY VERSE: LUKE 24:6
He is not here, but is risen!

WEEK 12

247. How did people mock Jesus while He was on the cross? (Luke 23:35–38)

A. He saved others; let Him save Himself if He is the Christ
B. If You are the King of the Jews, save Yourself
C. An inscription was written over Him in letters of Greek, Latin, and Hebrew: THIS IS THE KING OF THE JEWS.
D. All the above

248. After Jesus was crucified, what happened from the sixth hour to the ninth hour? (Luke 23:44)

A. There was wailing and great anguish
B. There was mourning
C. There was darkness over all the land
D. There was a great light across the world

249. Who was the good and just council member who asked Pilate for Jesus' body so he could bury Him? (Luke 23:50-51)

A. Joseph of Arimathea
B. Joseph of Galilee
C. Joseph the Nazarene
D. Joseph of Cupertino

WEEK 12 MEMORY VERSE: LUKE 24:6
He is not here, but is risen!

WEEK 12

250. Jesus appeared to two of His followers while they were walking to which town? (Luke 24:13)

A. Emmaus
B. Nazareth
C. Bethlehem
D. Washington

251. What did Jesus do when He appeared to the two followers on the road to Emmaus? (Luke 24:13–31)

A. He expounded to them in all the scriptures things concerning Himself
B. He did not reveal His true identity to them at first
C. He stayed a while with them, and after breaking bread together, He revealed His identity to them
D. All the above

252. What did Jesus tell His disciples to look at to prove it was really Him? (Luke 24:36–40)

A. His eyes
B. His soul
C. His Spirit
D. His hands and feet

WEEK 12 MEMORY VERSE: LUKE 24:6
He is not here, but is risen!

BONUS QUESTIONS

253. What food did Jesus eat with His disciples after His resurrection? (Luke 24:42)

A. Fish and bread
B. Broiled fish and honeycomb
C. Pigs feet
D. White lamb

254. Jesus told His disciples to stay in Jerusalem until what happened? (Luke 24:44–49)

A. They were endowed with power from on high
B. They were filled with the Holy Spirit/power from heaven
C. Both A and B
D. Christ's return

255. What happened after Jesus was resurrected and had finished speaking to His disciples? (Luke 24:50-51)

A. He blessed them
B. He was parted from them and carried up into heaven
C. He died and was resurrected again
D. Both A and B

WEEK 12 MEMORY VERSE: LUKE 24:6
He is not here, but is risen!

"

In Him I live and move and have my being (Acts 17:28)

"

Great job completing the week!

**Did you memorize the daily verse?
Test yourself by writing it here...**

_____

_____

_____

_____

_____

_____

**Use this space to draw a scene from the Bible or reflect
on something you learned, felt or experienced...**

Certificate of Completion

This Certificate Certifies That:

_____

Has Successfully Completed The Luke Workbook!

Flo & Grace

_____

PARENT/TEACHER SIGNATURE

PROJECT KINGDOM COME

WOULD YOU LIKE TO ACCEPT JESUS INTO YOUR HEART?

THE BIBLE SAYS:

If you confess with your mouth that Jesus is Lord and believe in your heart that God has raised Him from the dead, you will be saved
(Romans 10:9)

SAY THE PRAYER BELOW OUT LOUD AND BELIEVE IT IN YOUR HEART!

Dear Lord Jesus,
I know that I am a sinner, and I ask for Your forgiveness.
I believe You died for my sins and rose from the dead.
I repent of my sins and invite You to come into my heart and life.
I want to trust and follow You as my Lord and Savior. Help me to live for you for the rest of my life.
I am now a child of God, and I ask You to fill me with Your Holy Spirit.

In Jesus' Name I pray, Amen.

Congratulations!

If you have prayed this prayer, please let an adult know or send an email to mybibleworkbooks@gmail.com

1. C	13. B	25. B	37. C	49. C	61. C
2. C	14. B	26. C	38. A	50. C	62. B
3. C	15. B	27. C	39. B	51. C	63. C
4. B	16. B	28. D	40. A	52. A	64. C
5. C	17. B	29. A	41. A	53. B	65. C
6. B	18. C	30. A	42. A	54. D	66. C
7. C	19. B	31. B	43. C	55. C	67. B
8. B	20. A	32. B	44. B	56. B	68. A
9. B	21. C	33. B	45. B	57. C	69. C
10. C	22. C	34. A	46. D	58. C	70. A
11. B	23. C	35. B	47. C	59. C	71. B
12. D	24. B	36. A	48. B	60. C	72. B

73. B	85. C	97. C	109. B	121. A
74. D	86. D	98. B	110. C	122. B
75. A	87. D	99. C	111. C	123. B
76. C	88. A	100. D	112. D	124. B
77. C	89. B	101. A	113. C	125. B
78. D	90. A	102. D	114. B	126. A
79. A	91. B	103. C	115. A	127. B
80. A	92. C	104. C	116. A	128. C
81. A	93. B	105. D	117. B	129. D
82. D	94. D	106. A	118. B	130. B
83. B	95. D	107. A	119. D	131. A
84. B	96. D	108. C	120. A	132. C

133. B	145. D	157. D	169. D	181. A
134. D	146. D	158. D	170. D	182. C
135. D	147. D	159. B	171. B	183. B
136. D	148. B	160. D	172. C	184. B
137. D	149. D	161. D	173. D	185. B
138. D	150. C	162. D	174. D	186. A
139. A	151. B	163. C	175. C	187. C
140. B	152. A	164. A	176. B	188. B
141. A	153. D	165. A	177. A	189. D
142. C	154. C	166. D	178. D	190. A
143. A	155. D	167. D	179. D	191. B
144. C	156. B	168. C	180. A	192. D

193. C	205. C	217. B	230. A	243. C
194. C	206. C	218. D	231. A	244. A
195. D	207. B	219. A	232. A	245. C
196. D	208. C	220. D	233. C	246. D
197. D	209. C	221. C	234. D	247. D
198. C	210. A	222. A	235. D	248. C
199. A	211. A	223. C	236. D	249. A
200. D	212. C	224. B	237. C	250. A
201. D	213. A	225. A	238. D	251. D
202. D	214. C	226. A	239. B	252. D
203. A	215. D	227. B	240. C	253. B
204. B	216. D	228. A	241. B	254. C
		229. D	242. B	255. D

PLEASE GIVE US YOUR FEEDBACK!

Please send us your feedback on this workbook. We would love to hear what you enjoyed most, and ways you think it could be improved!

Please Send an email to: MyBibleWorkbooks@gmail.com, or leave us a comment on one of our social media pages.

MyBibleWorkbooks@gmail.com

Projectkingdomcome

Projectkingdomcome

SCAN ME

> And I am certain that God, who began the good work within you, will continue His work until it is finally finished on the day when Christ Jesus returns. Philippians 1:6

DRAW HERE

DRAW HERE